CW00409429

(

Cover image: Drinking scene on an image stone from Gotland, Courtesy of the Swedish Museum of National Antiquities, Stockholm

Dedication

I dedicate this book to my wonderful wife Rebbecca. You have helped me find my way back to building a Worthy Life, after I got lost.

I have loved you for a thousand years and will love you for a thousand more.

Thanks, and Acknowledgements

There are so many people to thank when you write and publish a book, and in writing this one I am no exception. So many people have helped me learn the information that I am sharing here with you, my wonderful readers. Actually, I will start with you, the person who has purchased my book and is now reading these words. Thank you very much for choosing my book, I hope you will learn something that will help you to live a Worthy Life.

I want to thank my family who taught me so much and continue to do so every day. My parents (love you Mum and Dad), Granny Boulton (the matriarch of our family as I grew up), my brother Matt (ya bloody ogre :P), my aunts and uncles, cousins, my in-laws, and of course my wife Rebbecca and my six wonderful and annoying children, I love you all.

Thank you to my friends who became my family, brothers and sisters of my heart, I love you all dearly. Especially Tony, who followed me home from school (and mum let me keep him). We have been friends and brothers for more than 30 years. Ally, you are more than Tony's wife, you are my sister always. Darren and Cher, Blade and Jaimie, Steve and Tahlisa, Leif and Spirit, Lynne and Krys, Tree, Kundra and the WA Spring Camp regulars.

Thanks to all the Heathens I have met, made friends with, shared mead and food with and discussed the Lore with. You have helped me shape my worldview and my world. This also includes all the Heathens I have interacted with online. Some of you have become online friends, some have not, but you have all given me something to think about and consider.

I need to say a special thank you to the SuperDads community. These men have been my encouragers, mentors, peer support and accountability group. Jarrod, the Founder of SuperDads, you are a friend and brother to me now. Adrian and Jeremy, both awesome coaches who helped me beat depression. Dean, Marty, Truey, Ray, Scott, Tim, Paul and the other SuperDads, thanks for being there for me.

Finally, a big thank you to my beta-readers, your feedback has been awesome and very encouraging. Bjarkan, Jarrod, Sonja, Tahlisa, Cher, Avalon, Claudie, Paulis, Berry, Terrence, Spirit, Clara, Tim, and Lynne, I am happy you all enjoyed my work.

You have helped me achieve this dream and goal of publishing my first book.

Special thanks must go to Cher Gottfried-Wilson, who has stepped up and taken on the role of editor. This book has been well polished thanks to her efforts. William Van Blaircum for his great work on the cover of my book, it is far better than any I could do myself. Lastly, to Eric Wodening for writing the foreword to my book. Your writings have helped shaped my view on Heathenry from the outset, I am highly honoured for your support of my book.

Foreword

Among the rituals practised in Heathendom, Sumbel numbers among the most important. To an outsider, Sumbel might simply appear to be a drinking ritual, but for a Heathen it is a ritual through which one places himself or herself in the flow of Wyrd, effectively linking the deeds of the past with those of the present. It is during Sumbel that oaths to perform various deeds are often made. Given that Sumbel is meant to link the past with the present, oaths taken during Sumbel should be taken very seriously.

Perhaps no better example of the seriousness of oaths made at Sumbel can be found than the poem *Beowulf*. In the poem (lines 499-558), Beowulf makes an oath to slay Grendel. Before making his oath, he boasts of past deeds, thus linking what he intends to do with what he has done in the past. King Hroðgar's þyle Unferð challenges Beowulf's oath. While the poem claims that Unferð was envious of Beowulf's fame, it seems likely that the þyle's challenge of Beowulf's oath served a purpose. Quite simply, he had to ensure that Beowulf was serious about his oath and that Beowulf intended to keep it.

While today's Heathen would not be making an oath to kill a monster such as Grendel, that does not make the oaths made during Sumbel any less serious. If an individual makes an oath that he or she will build a house before the end of the year, then he or she had better have that house built by the end of the year. If a person makes an oath that he or she will get a job in six months, then he or she had better have a job by the end of those six months. Because Sumbel links the deeds of the past with those of the present, words spoken in Sumbel have power. That means that any oaths taken during Sumbel have more power than oaths spoken at any other time. As serious as breaking an oath made outside of Sumbel can be, breaking an oath made during Sumbel can be even worse.

Of course, fulfilling oaths is not always a simple task, and even experienced Heathens could use help from time to time. A guide to help one keep his or her oaths and achieve what he or she sets out to do would be most useful. This book is just such a guide, incorporating what we known from the old lore with what we have learned more recently about improving oneself. Given the seriousness of making oaths at Sumbel, this would make it a most welcome addition to any Heathen's library.

Eric Wodening

Author of 'We Are Our Deeds'

January 2018

Rebuilding a Worthy Life

Many years ago, back in the late 1990's and early 2000's, I was a member of a Heathen Theod (tribe) or congregation. Every season, as part of our religious celebrations, we held a Sumbel. This was a time of success and good fortune for me. I was a leader in our religious community. I was working regularly, first as a cleaner, then as a Training and Placement Officer. Building respect within the greater community. I met the mother of my son, a woman I had hoped to marry. We had a boy together. We bought a home and were well on our way to buying an investment property. I had goals, dreams and modest ambitions, which I boasted of in Sumbel. I was achieving my modest goals, boasting of my successes and the successes of my Heathen kin. Now, things were not perfect, but I was living a life of worth.

This came to an end in 2004. Because of my then fiancé, I had a massive argument with my parents. In 2005, I quit my job, sold up everything and moved interstate with my son and his mother. The relationship with my partner had become strained.

Even though I joined another Heathen community, this one did not perform Sumbel on as regular a basis as my previous group. Between 2005 and 2007 I struggled to find employment and my relationship deteriorated further. In the beginning of 2007, my relationship with my son's mother finally ended and she left both my son and myself. I was saddled with debt and facing bankruptcy. I had managed to obtain casual employment as a disability support worker that allowed me to work whilst my son was in preschool. I managed to work my way out of debt and thus avoided bankruptcy. But, the pressures of being a single father to a young child and the stress of a mentally and emotionally demanding job took its toll. By mid-2008, I had a breakdown, was diagnosed with depression, and placed on medication.

I struggled over the next few years while trying to study a Bachelor of Arts doing a double major in Classical History and Linguistics, raise my son, look for work, deal with my depression, and a new relationship. My new partner didn't like the fact that I was raising my son as she believed all children belonged with their mothers, regardless. This was always a bone of contention in our relationship.

Unfortunately, we both suffered from depression and enabled the depressive behaviours that prevented our growth. We moved locations, got some work and I stopped studying my BA while continuing to struggle with my depression. I also stopped doing Sumbels and attending Blessings honouring my Gods. We mutually ended the relationship in early 2012, understanding that we were hampering each other's growth. With an economic downturn, my casual position disappeared, and I was unemployed once again.

In that same year, I met my current partner and now wife. I moved from South Australia to New South Wales to be with her and her family. As we became integrated as a family and dealt with the various health issues that are part of our family life, I continued to battle depression, self-harm and having thoughts of suicide. My self-esteem and self-worth were basically non-existent. With my beautiful lady's support and love I slowly started beating depression. In 2016, I joined a support group for fathers called SuperDads. With their support, and that of my family, I finally defeated my long-term depression after eight years of struggle.

As I started regaining a more positive mindset, I started meditating more and making offerings to my Gods once again. I realised that what I had stopped doing and was missing in my life was the power of Ritual. I also remembered back to the time when my life had purpose and I was achieving my goals. I recognised that one of the rituals which helped me build a worthy life was the ritual known as Sumbel. I have started performing Sumbel once again with a small group of friends. With these actions, I am again feeling connected to the flow of Wyrd and my Maegan building up within me. My life is turning around and once more becoming a worthy life.

I am writing this book to share my knowledge with others. To help you to build a life of worth. Whether you are starting at the bottom (like I have done), you are having some successes but need a boost, or you want to harness the power of ritual to further enhance your achievements in life, I hope my experience can be a guide. I also intend to continue helping myself in writing this book. I am mapping out what I need to do to carry on rebuilding a worthy life. I want my path to be a positive role for my children to emulate, unlike the self-destructive and depressed person that I had been. In finishing this project, I will have completed a Sumbel oath to write and publish my first book. I already know that it will not be my last. It is my hope that others will join me on the quest to build (or rebuild in my case) a worthy life.

A note to my Heathen readers. This book is designed to help your kindreds to achieve their goals and fulfil the oaths made at Sumbel. Yes, I admit I have adapted the Ritual of Sumbel to suit my purposes for this book. This is not to replace your own traditions regarding Sumbel, rather it is a supplement to your own traditions. This can help further encourage the doing of deeds, which has been a core of the modern Heathen movement for at least the past 25 years that I have been a Heathen. After all, Heathenry is about doing more than believing. Get out, do some deeds and create a worthy life. Aid your kindred in becoming even more honourable people who have mighty deeds for your Skalds to sing.

To my non-Heathen readers, this book is also for you. From it you can learn about a powerful ritual that has its origins in a tribal culture that goes back thousands of years. This ritual has withstood the test of time and has helped countless generations live worthy lives. I have done my best to keep the complex concepts that are central to the mindset and cultural tribal beliefs that we modern practitioners call Heathenry simple easy to understand. Sumbel can and will add a depth of intentionality and significance to your goal setting practices that is hard to achieve without the use of ritual. The information in this book can become the basis of creating a powerful new tradition in your support network or brainstorming groups. One that takes advantage of the best research into human behaviour and self-improvement and blends it with a timeless ritual.

I would love to hear about your successes in building a worthy life using the power of Sumbel. Contact me at (thom.burton@outlook.com) and like my Facebook author's page (www.facebook.com/buildaworthylife) for updates on my writing and inspiration. Don't forget to leave feedback for my book on Amazon.

Section One

Developing an Anglo-Norse Mindset

Who are the Anglo-Norse?

I believe that there are two distinct tribes that existed during the first millennium that best encapsulates this spirit of endurance, strength and thriving against all odds that is the source of inspiration for me and my desire to share my knowledge with you.

The Anglii, were a tribe from the area of the modern border between Germany and Denmark. In the 3rd century they, along with the Jutes, Saxons, Frisii and others, took to the sea and raided the coasts at the north-western edge of the Roman Empire. For 200 years the Anglii harried the coasts of Roman Britain and Gaul. Then, as the Roman empire withdrew their legions in the fifth century, they started to invade and settle South-East Britain. Over the course of the next few centuries they formed a new nation; Angle-land, or as we know it England. The Norse were the people of North-western Scandinavia, who in the 8th Century boarded boats and raided Britain and Europe. For 300 years the Norse (along with the Danes and Swedes) raided, explored and settled in most of Europe, from Russia and Byzantium in the east to Greenland and North America in the west. Today we remember these Norsemen as the Vikings. For simplicity's sake, I have chosen to combine their names and cultures into a single body; the Anglo-Norse.

These two vibrant peoples had similar languages, cultures and religions. During the Pagan period of European history, they worshipped similar Gods and Goddesses, known to us as the Aesir and Vanir. The language of both peoples are offshoots of the Germanic branch of the language tree known as the Indo-European family by linguists. Their poetry, warrior culture, desire to achieve greatness, rituals and what historians call 'mead-hall' culture was also similar. Even the structure of their societies shared common elements.

As you may have guessed, the Anglii and the Norse are only two out of the hundreds of tribes that lived in Northern Europe. These tribes shared a similar language (as mentioned above) and similar beliefs. The names of several may be familiar to you; Saxons, Vandals, Danes, Visigoths, Ostrogoths, Franks, Burgundians, Swedes, Geats. Others are not so well known; Heruli, Alemani, Cherusci, Seubi, Chatti, Lombards. In his book entitled "Germania," the

Roman Historian Tacitus listed many tribes, all of them part of the Germanic language family tree and all of them worshipped the Gods known today as the Aesir and Vanir. These tribes, collectively known as the Germanic tribes (thanks to Tacitus), lived across Northern Europe over a time span of some 3-4000 years, their tribal cultural practices ended by the process of Christianisation that ended in the 13th century. These tribes practiced the ritual known as Sumbel, albeit in a slightly different manner to the one I describe in this book. Now you may be thinking, "All this is interesting Thom, thanks for the history lesson, but what does this mean to me today? Why should these cultures matter to any of us living more than a thousand years later?"

Quite simply, within their surviving poems, sagas, myths and histories are keys to help us unlock their strengths; courage, wisdom, fortitude and an inner strength to achieve goals and accomplish deeds. I will guide you in learning what it takes to live a worthy life according to the practices of the Anglo-Norse. I will teach you the two-part view of fate; Orlog (from the Norse) is how the present and future were built upon layers of past actions. In understanding this, we can see how practicing and building regular habits will change the shape of our own lives. Then I will teach you about the Anglo-Norse concepts of strength. Strength (Thews in Old English) is not just the physical muscular strength, but includes mental fortitude, customs and traditions, as well as familial relationships. Finally, I will explore one of the most powerful rituals that the Anglo-Norse shared, The Sumbel. This is a ritual in which participants state what deed, or goal they are going to achieve. You will learn how to perform and harness the power of this ritual to enhance your own goal-setting practices and 'lay' your successes into the fabric of your Wyrd and Orlog to help shape your life and the lives of those around you.

Wyrd and Orlog; The Anglo-Norse Concepts of Fate

Who has heard of the phrase (or variation of) 'who you are today is based on the actions you took five years ago'? It is a common concept within motivational circles. With the idea that what you do today will shape the person you will be in five years' time. This is not a new or modern thought. It is based in the ancient beliefs of the Anglo-Norse Heathens view of fate, or as they knew it, Wyrd and Orlog. Wyrd is the past actions that are brought forward to shape the present. Not all actions are equal, however. Stronger and more powerful actions will have a greater impact than smaller, weaker actions. For example, changing the colour of your hair, whilst having an impact immediately, doesn't really impact the person you will be 20, 40 or 60 years' time. Moving to a new house on the other hand, particularly moving a great distance such as interstate, will have a greater impact over the course of your life.

The Anglo-Norse used a complex metaphor revolving around a well, a tree, water and three sisters. Very basically, our actions fall from the leaves of the tree like dew drops. Some fall to the ground and are lost, some fall from the tree and into the Well of Wyrd. They mix into the waters of this bubbling, natural spring. Next, the Three sisters called the Norns, collect the muddy water. Then, after performing specific rituals, water the tree. Through this process, powerful actions then feed the tree of life (Yggdrasil as it is called by the Anglo-Norse). This tree holds everything, the Gods, the universe and us. From this, we can see that the ancient Anglo-Norse believed that their personal significant actions helped shape the fabric of the very universe itself. However, like a drop of water into a pond, our deeds ripple outwards. Firstly, we are most affected, then those closest to us, then so on out to the edges of the pond.

You might think that our actions shaping the universe are a bit far-fetched, and that is fine, but think of the actions of some people who have changed our world. The actions of a Scotsman called James Watt led to the Industrial revolution. The actions of two men, the Wright Brothers, changed the way we travel around the world. History is full of examples of ordinary people whose very actions shaped the history of our world and the way we do things today.

How can we ensure that our actions (deeds as the Anglo-Norse called them) will have the greatest impact on us and on those around us? How can we make sure our goals for ourselves, when fulfilled, will have the greatest impact? Through the ritual of Sumbel, and building habits of repeated actions, we can lay our deeds into the Well of Wyrd and from there they can form layers, shaping our Orlog. Small and consistent habits, with an effective ritual, can shape our lives. Our present is shaped by the actions taken in the past.

Orlog

Now you might be thinking what does a thousand-year-old concept of fate have to do with us today? Well, I am going to show you. The Anglo-Norse fate wasn't a fixed and immutable concept. Yes, there are some things that you cannot change. For example, you can't change where you were born nor, can you change who your birth parents are. But there are things you do which can change your fate. The Old

Norse referred to fate as Orlog, pronounced roughly as 'or-lay'. Orlog translates more directly as 'primal layers' which better describes what Orlog is rather than the word fate. Orlog is the layers of our actions and deeds over periods of time. However, only significant deeds leave enough of an imprint in the layers of time to affect the future.

The Anglo-Norse believed that they could shape the future by laying deeds into the Well of Wyrd (Old English word for fate) that was used to feed and water the World Tree, which grew and held all things in the cosmos. With this mindset, a goal promised and boasted of in Sumbel could affect the evolution and growth, not just of the individual, but of the entire cosmos. This is the power of the ancient ritual of Sumbel which helped the Anglo-Norse to explore, expand and change European history while shaping our modern western culture. Using the power of Sumbel, we can 'lay' our goals into our own Orlogs and thus change the shape of our future.

Let me show you, with this easy example. Here I have some pieces of cloth borrowed from my wife's stash, some paperclips, a couple of pencils and some blocks. The cloth represents layers of time, the paperclips are the everyday things that happen in life such as bills to pay, getting the kids off to school, going to work, running late and washing the dishes. The pencils represent life changing events. Things like the death of a loved one, moving from one home to another or a change of career. The things that have a big impact on our lives. Finally, we have the blocks. These represent those goals and deeds we have achieved and spoke of in Sumbel.

Let us start laying out our example of Orlog. I will drop a few paperclips down, then I will put a pencil down to show us starting a new job. Lastly, I put down one small block to show our Sumbel oath to get a job. Over this all I place a piece of cloth to show a layer of time passing by. Let's repeat this process a couple of more times. A few paperclips showing the pain of driving to work, and paying the rent, no pencil this time because nothing major has happened, and finally another block on top of where the previous block was, because we hold Sumbels at the same time each year. This Sumbel perhaps, we celebrate a personal goal of reading every day. Another layer of time, some more paperclips of necessary tasks, again no pencil, and another block representing our Sumbel. Now I add a fourth layer, with a Sumbel, some everyday annoyances, and another life changing pencil to represent falling in love. Last, I add a fifth layer with just the Sumbel ritual and some paperclips of 'life.' After five layers, we can see that the paperclips of everyday life have hardly made any impact at all. The pencils of life events have left an impact that slowly lessen over time. The blocks of the Sumbel ritual along with the goals and deeds spoken of have left a lasting and permanent change to the Orlog of our life.

With this visual example, you can clearly see the power of a regular ritual, habit or routine on our lives over time. Sumbel adds emphasis, motivation, impetus and the power of ritual to your goals.

The Anglo-Norse Concept of Time

The Anglo-Norse didn't see time the way we do today. We see time as being linear, going from the past through to the present and into the future. The march of time is always forwards and never goes back. As a society, we focus more on the future than the present, and consider anyone who thinks or concerns themselves with the past as anachronistic, 'stuck in the past' or worse. Thinking about the past is often seen as a waste of time. Yet for the Anglo-Norse the past was alive, it was real, and it shaped the present. For these ancient peoples' time was cyclical, it turned like the seasons do, and like a stairway or spring with each turning of time laying upon the past. The present is constantly becoming. The Anglo-Norse personified the present with the Norn (one of the sisters who watered the tree of life I spoke of before) Werthende (Old English, roughly pronounced Worth-end-eh) or Verdandi (in Old Norse, roughly pronounced Ver-than-di). Her name means 'to twist' or 'to turn', like time itself does. Another meaning is 'to become', but what does the present become? What can the current moment turn into? There is only one thing that the present can become, and that is the past.

As you will remember from our discussion on Orlog and Wyrd, the past consists of layers of time in which significant, and repeated, actions continued to shape the present. It is as the motivational speakers say, "who you are today is based on everything you did five years ago." My choice to try internet dating five years ago (2012) led me to be a father of six children living in a different state (I moved from SA to NSW) today (2017). Even the actions of our parents, grandparents and ancestors can shape who we are to a certain extent. Using myself as an example again, I was born in Australia because my parents moved here, from England in the 1960's. You will also remember the examples of deeds done by people in the past that continue to influence our lives today. We live with the influences of the past affecting us every day. Clothes, cooking, electricity, internal combustion engines, aircraft, even the internet, are all items created by someone in the past.

The Anglo-Norse did not really have sense of the future as we do. For them the future was based upon Debt and Obligation. The debt we must pay for the actions, or inactions, we take today. We have an obligation to fulfil our oaths made at Sumbel, to complete the goals we set ourselves before our friends and family. All things have a price and that price must be paid. Scyld (Old English roughly pronounced as shield) or Skuld in Old Norse (roughly pronounced as skooled) is that price. When we meet our Scyld, our debts and obligations are rewarded. If we fail to do so, then we are punished (another meaning of Scyld is guilt). That may sound a bit harsh or impersonal, and in a way, it is. However, think of it like taking out a bank loan. We borrow money from the bank to buy something thus incurring Scyld to the bank. When we pay out our debt, we keep our item, say a house, and that house becomes our reward, making it easier to borrow money from the bank in the future. If we fail to pay out the loan, we lose the house and it becomes harder to borrow money from the bank again. This is our punishment for not fulfilling our debt and obligation, our Scyld, to the bank. The Anglo-Norse viewed the future as the debts and obligations incurred by our words and actions in the present.

With this basic understanding of the Anglo-Norse mindset regarding time, how can we harness the past (Wyrd) to turn our present (Werthende) into the kind of future where our debts and obligations (Scyld) are the ones we want to pay? I believe that the Anglo-Norse had the answer in their ritual called Sumbel. As we have learned earlier, we shape who we are by the deeds we do on a regular basis. Consistently performing actions on a regular basis will create 'bumps' in our Orlog that will change the shape of our lives. How often should we plan on holding a Sumbel? Did the Anglo-Norse measure time in a way that we can harness today to create goals and the habits to achieve them around? Quite simply yes, they did.

The Anglo-Norse used a lunar calendar to reckon their years (like the Chinese still do). Each year consists of 12 lunar months, with a thirteenth month added during the summer every 2-3 years. This cycle is known to astronomers as the Metonic cycle, named for the Greek astronomer Meton. The Metonic cycle lasts for nineteen years before repeating itself. Now, nineteen years is a bit long to be setting goals for, beyond a general idea of what we would like to accomplish. After all, we are probably only going to live through around four to six of these cycles in our lifetimes (5x19=95 years). Whilst this cycle is interesting and helps us understand the complexity of the Anglo-Norse lunar calendar, it is not quite as useful for setting goals to achieve deeds.

However, there was a practice in ancient Sweden (culturally like the Norse in ancient times) where they would hold a festival (called the Great Disting) every eight years at a place called Uppsala. This eight-year cycle is known to astronomers as the octaeteris. It was a cycle of the moon returning to the exact same place relative to the sky. This tended to occur approximately every nine lunar years. A number sacred to the Anglo-Norse. Whilst this eight-year period is longer than the common five-year plan used today, it does fit within natural observable events which the Anglo-Norse used to reckon time. This eight-year period is ideal for those of us developing an Anglo-Norse mindset to use for our long-term goal setting and strategizing.

Shorter term, the Anglo-Norse recognised the solar year very similar to what we use today. The year generally started and ended with the Winter Solstice. Yule was a sacred time for the Anglo-Norse Heathen, as they celebrated the dying of the old year and birth of the new one. Many of our Christmas and New Year's traditions are based on these customs. A year is great for planning short to medium term goals. As they also used a Lunar calendar, we could choose to set our plans according to that. We do need to understand that every second or third year would consist of thirteen lunar months rather than twelve.

One of the most important cycles of time for the Anglo-Norse was the turning of the seasons. The Anglo-Norse generally recognised the four seasons as we know them today. Often, they were celebrated at the Solstices and Equinoxes, or the full moon after them (a bit like Easter today). It is this roughly three-month cycle that is of greatest use to us. This length of time is ideal for developing new habits to help us achieve the goals we set at Sumbel. It is the ideal time to hold a Sumbel, as well. There is no hard and fast rule here, and we do have to be adaptable to family commitments. For example, the solstice in December is usually around the 21st and close to Christmas, a busy time for pretty much everyone in Western society. However, the Sumbel ritual could easily be added to your Christmas or holiday traditions. The same can be said for the equinox in March, which is close to Easter.

The only other main measure of time that we need to consider is the lunar cycle. A period which lasts for around 29 days. The Anglo-Norse lunar month runs from new moon to new moon. Generally, we take the sighting of the first crescent after new moon as the start of the new month, or monath in Old English. These short periods are a great for checking your progress with a new habit that you are trying to build. For those of us developing an Anglo-Norse mindset, the seasonal cycles upon which we base our Sumbel rituals are of greater importance. It is good to check your progress on this monthly basis, making sure that you are on track and whether you should tweak your action plan to complete your goal.

A Worthy Life According to the Anglo-Norse

The Anglo-Norse did not primarily seek wealth and fame for their own sakes. They saw both wealth and fame (renown) as by-products of living a worthy life. To live a worthy life was the goal of the Anglo-Norse, a life worth remembering by those who followed. As the Norse proverb says; It is better to be without money than without honour. The meaning is clear: being honourable, having a good reputation and being a person of worth is more important than being rich. The Havamal, which is a collection of sayings and proverbs from the Viking age, says often that wisdom is better than wealth. Those of us who seek to develop an Anglo- Norse mindset need to bear in mind that our primary focus should be on living a worthy life rather than foolishly chasing money.

But what exactly does that mean? What is a worthy life, what does it mean to us today and how can we live a worthy life according to the principles of the Anglo-Norse?

Let us explore this concept of a worthy life. Even the ancients knew that not everyone could be a mighty hero like Beowulf or Harald Hardrada, but they did expect everyone to live up to a certain standard. The average warrior (Duguth in Old English) was expected to be honourable, loyal, strong, a capable fighter, generous, hard-working, reasonably knowledgeable, capable of contributing to the well-being of your family and being an active member of your tribe. These virtues, or Thews, were the cornerstones of living a worthy life according to the Anglo-Norse. So, let us explore these Thews in greater depth.

Firstly, I am going to start with the overall term that I have previously introduced you to, the word Thews. **Thews** means strength. This is not just physical strength but also strength of purpose, strength of will, and strength of spirit. In modern terms, Thews could be considered all those things that go with promoting self-empowerment. Things like virtues and ethics, living a life with passion and purpose. Having self-respect, self-love and good self-esteem is all part of living a worthy life. Thews has the additional meaning of customs and traditions. Those regular practices that keep a family, clan, tribe and nation working together in a cohesive manner. These customs and traditions give meaning, purpose and worth to our everyday lives. As you can see, to live a worthy life, one must live a thewful life which is a life rich in customs, purpose and traditions -such as Sumbel- and practicing the virtues that improve our self-esteem and self-worth.

There are two virtues that the Anglo Norse saw as more important than wealth, so let us examine those next. The first of these is **Wisdom**. We often hear or read in self-help and motivational books, speeches, etc., the importance of learning every day. Spend 15 to 30 minutes a day reading to feed your mind. Seeking knowledge is a great virtue in and of itself. However, just learning about things is not enough. We need to apply that knowledge so that we may know it. Finally, there is sharing what we have learned with others which means we have truly gained wisdom in that area. There are vast differences between knowing about stuff through reading or watching a YouTube clip, applying that knowledge in your own life, and having enough knowledge to teach others about the topic.

In the religion of the Anglo-Norse, Odin is considered the God of Wisdom. He wandered the various worlds seeking knowledge wherever he could. But he didn't just stop with acquiring that knowledge, he then used it to help the Gods in their constant war against the Thurses (giants) of chaos and destruction. He taught what he knew to the other Gods and to humanity so that we could all benefit from his knowledge, applying it in our lives. In this, Odin is the perfect role model for the virtue of wisdom. Learn something (such as how-to self-publish a book), apply the knowledge in your own life (write and publish a book) and finally teach others what you know (create a course, either formal or informal, on self-publishing).

The second virtue which was considered more important than wealth was honour. **Honour** is a bit of a tricky thing to define. It is quite a personal concept that can mean different things to different people. The meaning can also change based upon different cultures as well. Basically, it is doing what is morally right according to your cultural traditions. In other words, Thewful behaviour. Honour is your self-esteem and respect for yourself, your family and your community and the way others treat you with respect. For the Anglo-Norse, it meant keeping your word, meeting your debts and obligations (remember

Scyld?), fulfilling your goals as you boasted/promised to do at Sumbel. Your honour is your reputation and your personal moral compass. Honour is increased by doing what is right, living in accordance to the Thews of the Anglo-Norse mindset. It is lessened when you do unworthy deeds -those things that are against the Anglo-Norse Thews- that which is harmful to yourself, your family and your community. To quote a friend of mine, Dan R. Miller, 'that which is beneficial to the wholeness and health of the chain of generations is good (or honourable).'

Loyalty is next. In Anglo-Norse society, loyalty to one's leaders and family was key to the entire culture. For those of us developing an Anglo-Norse mindset, we need to be loyal to our friends, family and our purpose in life. A loyal friend is often called a true friend. This is because to the Anglo-Norse loyalty and truth/trust are intertwined. To be true to yourself, your purpose, your friends and family means sticking with them in good times and in bad. The loyal person helps a friend or family member when they desperately need help. They are also there in the good times sharing in the successes of life. The Havamal states that the tree which stands alone on the plain will wither and die, so too will a person with no one to love. Without the bonds of loyalty to support, sustain and encourage you, it is easy to fall prey to hopelessness, loneliness, low self-esteem, low self-worth and depression.

Generosity it the next virtue for a Thewful life. Sharing what you have with your friends and family was the norm for the Anglo-Norse. If your family failed to thrive, so did you. Be generous with those whom you are loyal. Gift-giving builds the bonds of friendship and loyalty like nothing else. This is what the Anglo-Norse religious rituals were, giving gifts in the form of weapons, treasures, food and drink to the Gods and Ancestors. When we toast the Gods and ancestors/heroes in Sumbel, we are giving them the gift of being remembered and honoured, as well as the drink that we share in Sumbel. Let us be clear, gifts do not have to be great or expensive. Indeed, the Havamal tells us that it is better not to give at all than to give too much. Buying a meal, shouting a drink, tickets to a movie, something that you have made, or even giving your time by helping elderly or disabled relatives and friends are all worthy gifts.

Hospitality is a part of generosity yet deserves to be explored a bit. For the ancient Anglo-Norse, there were no hotels to stay in when travelling. Hospitality could well be the difference between life and freezing to death on the side of the road. Being willing to take someone in for a night or two was considered an important part of being generous. The host was expected to provide what they could share, food and a warm dry place to sleep. The guest was expected to be courteous, provide some entertainment (in those days tell of the news they learned on their travels) and, if they were staying more than one night, give some help around the home of the host.

Now we come to **hard work**. For the Anglo-Norse this thew was the difference between death and survival. They got up every day, ploughed, planted and harvested crops, repaired buildings and equipment, cut firewood, spun fibres into threads, wove threads into cloth and made clothes. You get the idea, pretty much everything needed to survive. Nowadays, we do not have to do most of those basic survival skills (except as an enjoyable hobby). But, we still have housework to do. We have dishes, laundry, vacuuming, sweeping and gardens to tend. Many of us have jobs to go to and children to raise. We also have goals to fulfil. We need to work at these things if we want to live a worthy life. Laziness is unworthy and will lower our sense of self-worth. Being lazy will not help us live a worthy life nor will it build our honour and a good reputation with our families and communities. Every day you need to take care of your regular routines and work towards fulfilling your goals that you boasted of at Sumbel.

Being a **capable warrior** was considered an important virtue for the Anglo-Norse. Even their women were expected to know how to defend themselves and their homes. For us, the chances of being raided or attacked are quite slim. We do not get into our boats for a bout of summer raiding like the Angles and Norse did. Our lives are safe in a way that they would never have known so being a capable warrior is not as important as it used to be. Depending on where you live, you could still face dangers from criminals, drug addicts, drunken louts and other unthewful folk. Learning how to defend yourself and your family in such situations is still important. Consider getting instruction in combatives, learn a martial art. If you want to better understand the Anglo-Norse mindset investigate Historical European Martial Arts (HEMA). HEMA investigates, interprets and trains in various weapons and armour used in medieval Europe. HEMA practitioners primarily use training manuals written in the 13th to 19th centuries. There are plenty of books, YouTube channels, websites, Facebook pages and even training schools dedicated to the study of HEMA.

With **strength**, we come full circle in our discussion of living a worthy life. As I said at the outset, strength is not just 'I can lift heavy things' physical strength, although that is a part of it. Strength includes everything we have discussed. Strength of purpose, strength of mind, strength of spirit and the strength of living a worthy life. Now, I do want to touch on the purely physical aspects of strength here. As we have learned, the Anglo-Norse needed to be physically strong to deal with the everyday tasks of survival in medieval times. A struggle that we in our modern western society do not have to face. However, there is much to be said about being physically fit. This is something for which we should all strive. Being fit and healthy will help us to achieve our goals (and could even be a goal that we pursue), help us to be loyal friends (by being able to help in times of need, like moving furniture) and provide for our family (growing food in our garden, or a physically demanding job).

In doing all you can to live by these Thews, you will further develop an Anglo-Norse mindset. This helps the health and wholeness of the chain of generations of your family, and ensures you live a worthy life. In the end, a worthy life; one that touches the lives of others in a positive manner and will be remembered long after we die, is the best we can hope for. I will finish with the words of the Havamal; "Cattle die, kinsmen die, even you will someday die. I know of one thing that never dies, how each of us is remembered."

Section Two

Harnessing the Power of Sumbel

The Ritual of Sumbel

We have finally reached the core purpose of my writing, the Ritual of Sumbel. Now you may be asking, "Thom, I do not believe in those Gods that the Anglo-Norse did, I am (insert the name of your belief system here). Can I use the Anglo-Norse mindset and the Ritual of Sumbel to help me?" The answer to that is, absolutely. In the surviving poems and sagas, we see Christians living with an Anglo-Norse mindset and using Sumbel to achieve their goals and living a worthy life. Three examples of Christians who did this are Beowulf, Harald Hardrada and Haakon the Good. Of these both Harald and Haakon were actual historical people. Haakon was King of Norway in the middle of the Tenth century until he died in 961CE (AD). Harald Hardrada was a Commander of the Varangian Guard in Constantinople before becoming King of Norway in 1047CE. Harald later died in the year 1066 when he invaded England. Beowulf is more than likely a fictional character and is best known from the poem bearing his name. This poem, a masterpiece of Anglo-Saxon poetry, is one of the key sources explaining the ritual of Sumbel. It was in this ritual that Beowulf boasted (set the goal) to kill the monster Grendel with his bare hands.

As you have seen, the mindset of the ancient Anglo-Norse is different from the modern western mindset, although there are still traces of the ancients' thought processes in our western culture. It is also rather different from the mindset of Christianity, as Wyrd was held supreme even over the Christian God. Beowulf ended his boast with the words 'Wyrd shall go as she wills.' Meaning that, despite his boast and skill, Wyrd could go against him if that was his fate; even if he had God on his side. So, whilst the Heathen religion of the ancient North Europeans will flow best with the Anglo-Norse mindset, one does not have to be Heathen to develop the same mindset using Sumbel as the ritual for goal setting.

Let us now move on to the ritual of Sumbel itself. What is it, how often should we do it and how do we go about performing this ritual? I have already discussed how often we should perform Sumbel when I discussed the Anglo-Norse concepts of time. Ideally, we should hold a Sumbel four times per year in tune with the seasons. One of the benefits of this is that it fits well within the time it takes to develop a habit. According to the British Behavioural Insights Team it takes between 18 and 254 days to create a new habit, depending upon the individual and the complexity of the new habit. Sumbels are held roughly every 90 days, making them ideal points to review your progress regarding building regular habits to achieve your goals.

A Sumbel is a ritual where people gather together to honour their Gods and boast of their ancestors or heroes, before making oaths to achieve specific goals. The Anglo-Norse used to gather in the Hall of their chieftains or kings for Sumbel. As we do not have either chieftains or kings, we can gather at the home of a designated person within the group that will be taking part in the Sumbel ritual. Sumbel is a social event and it needs a group of people for it to be successful. These people will be your peer support, brainstorming and accountability group. Ideally, they will be close friends and family that are also seeking to improve their lives through developing an Anglo-Norse mindset by using the ritual of Sumbel. In performing the ritual of Sumbel with them, you will be linking your Wyrd with theirs. The purpose of Sumbel is to help lay your deeds and goals into the Well of Wyrd and from there help shape the growth of all involved and associated with the ritual.

The Sumbel, as we shall use it, consists of four rounds of ritualized drinking. This is not some drinking bout designed to get drunk as quick as possible. Getting drunk at Sumbel is bad form and unthewful. Sumbel is a highly sacred ritual where one speaks over the horn or drinking vessel to help shape their Wyrd. The Anglo-Norse traditionally used mead as the ritual drink for Sumbel. Mead is a sweet alcoholic beverage that is brewed from a mixture of yeast, water and honey. This can become quite a strong beverage with an alcoholic content of between 12-20%. This is equivalent to most ordinary and fortified wines. However, we do not need to use mead for a successful Sumbel. Ales and ciders are a good alcoholic substitute to mead and are also traditional. For non-alcoholic options, apple juice mixed with honey is very good, or apple juice on its own. Milk could also be used as an alternative. Apples were the sacred fruit for the Anglo-Norse which represented wisdom, health, longevity, love, fertility and beauty. Milk was considered a special drink, being linked with the original cow Audhumbla at the creation of the worlds in Anglo-Norse mythology. Let common sense and group consensus be the guide when it comes to the drink chosen for Sumbel. Milk is no good for vegans or those with a lactose intolerance for example. Nor is alcohol an option for minors and reformed alcoholics.

The first round is dedicated to the Gods, one will call on and briefly honour a specific God or Goddess whom they wish to aid them to achieve their goal. This is often a God that you have an affinity for, or one that you wish to see and hear you. This would be a God that you believe in. If you are an atheist or have no connection with a specific deity, you would drink to your own personal strength and luck. That is your own self-worth.

The second round is generally a boast of a prominent ancestor or a worthy hero. The idea is to call upon the strength of the person's Maegan (spiritual luck) to support your endeavours. You are also helping write their deeds and memories into the web of Wyrd. For the Anglo-Norse, the Ancestors could help them from beyond the grave. They could visit in dreams and provide encouragement and guidance to the living. The spiritual strength of the ancestors was passed on to the living, giving them extra support to continue with their goals. This increases the health and wholeness of the chain of generations and builds up the worth of family lines.

The third round is a boast of your own deeds. Something you have achieved in your past which you are proud of. Showcase your skills, whether it something you made, a course completed, reciting a poem, singing a song you have learned, speaking the language you have been learning fluently (with a translation for those who are listening) or even losing weight. Embellishing you story is acceptable, but not outright lying (a friend of mine once described buying steaks from a supermarket in terms of hunting, for example). It is good to entertain those sharing in this ritual with your words.

The fourth round is where you pledge to do something. This is when you make your goal public and accountable before your peer group. This could be small like cleaning out a messy room or shed, finding out about courses available on a subject you are interested in, or a song or poem you would like to learn. You could go bigger by pledging to find a new job, buying a house, completing a university degree, starting a business or writing a book. You may want to give a timeframe to achieve this goal, as well. It is always best to end your boast to achieve the goal or deed with the words "Wyrd shall weave as she wills." This phrase allows for uncontrollable and unpredictable events that may disrupt your plans. You may not be able to attend the planned marathon if you're in hospital after a car accident, for example.

The leader, or host, of the Sumbel (either the host or chosen group member for this role) has the right to challenge your pledge. They may ask what you have done to help achieve this goal, get you to explain previous skills that you have which will help you. Be prepared to answer honestly. For example, if you are buying a house, you may be asked about deposit money, getting a bank loan, where you plan to buy and other questions. This is not to put you off or put you down, but to help you think through your pledge to achieve the goal. When challenged, you can outline the steps you plan to take in achieving your goal and talk about the first habit that you plan to implement in helping you achieving it. For example, if your goal is to write a book, you could say that each day after the kids are in bed you will spend one-hour writing. You will have set a plan of what and when you are going to do your activity and that will help you towards your goal.

If you are not about to undertake a new project, you can do a couple of different things in the fourth round. Firstly, you could speak of your progress on your long-term project. This increases the chance of laying your deed into the Well of Wyrd and having it shape your personal Orlog. The second option is to boast of the achievements of another person at the Sumbel. This has a few benefits; you are acknowledging the successes of your friends, you are boosting their confidence in their abilities and you are strengthening the bonds of friendship. You are also increasing the probability of the deed being woven into the Wyrd of everyone present. Finally, you could tell a story, recite a poem or otherwise entertain the group.

The Tools and Roles of Sumbel

Now that we have discussed what a Sumbel is, it is time to discuss the tools needed, and the roles required in performing this powerful ritual to enhance our goal setting. The tools that you will need are; a bowl, a drinking horn, mead, a small ladle, some where to put the various items, and enough seats for everyone to sit in a rough circle. There are also three key roles that need to be filled for a Sumbel to run smoothly. These roles are the Sumbel Giver, Ale (or Cup) Bearer and the Thyle.

Mead – this is the ritual drink. As discussed earlier, mead is an alcoholic drink brewed from honey. Along with ale, mead is the traditional drink used by the ancient Anglo-Norse for Sumbel. However, other options can be used if you do not wish to use an alcoholic beverage. These include Apple juice, milk, or honey mixed with water or apple juice. Cider, both the alcoholic and non-alcoholic varieties are also good options. For ease, I will continue to use the word mead for the drink consumed during Sumbel.

Drinking Horn – the Anglo-Norse used a cow horn as a drinking vessel for all their rituals. Those that have survived are actually very beautiful items. However, if you have an issue with drinking from a horn (if you are vegan for example) then it is perfectly acceptable to use a cup, goblet or glass to drink from. Ideally the drinking vessel (like all the tools) should be dedicated specifically for the Ritual of Sumbel, this will add extra depth and meaning to the ritual. The horn (I will continue to use the term horn for ease of writing) is the sacred vessel that carries the waters to, and from, the Well of Wyrd.

Bowl and Ladle - I will address these two items together as they work together during the Sumbel. The bowl represents the Well of Wyrd. That sacred place where all our actions go to be laid within our Orlog, and from there shape our lives and the lives of those connected to us. After the end of each round, the leftover mead in the horn is poured into the bowl by the Ale-bearer. This is our words being poured into the depths of the Well. The ladle is then used to pour some of the mead back into the horn which represents our words and deeds coming back to influence us. The horn is then topped up with more mead for the next round. The bowl will need to be large enough to hold all the excess mead from each of the four rounds of Sumbel. Like the horn, natural materials should be used for the bowl and ladle.

You will need to have a place to put the horn (when not being used), bowl, ladle and mead out during the Sumbel. A small coffee table will work for this. If possible, the table also needs to be specific for Sumbel, although this is not as necessary for the horn, bowl and ladle. If you are lucky (or crafty), the table could double as a storage space for the tools when not in use. A chest could also be used for storage and as a table if it is not too low for the Ale-bearer.

Seating - To sit at Sumbel is how participating in the ritual is described in the surviving descriptions of the Anglo-Norse sources. Having a place for everyone to sit is essential to conducting a successful Sumbel ritual. Everyone needs a place to sit in reasonable comfort. Lounges, armchairs, dining chairs or folding chairs are all good options. The room used for Sumbel will also need to be large enough to fit everyone. Technological devices such as phones, computers, tablets, televisions, and stereo systems should all be turned off. They will distract from the importance of the ritual and the words being spoken. It is also recommended that the number of people attending the Sumbel be somewhere between three and twenty. Know exactly how many will be attending the Sumbel and provide the appropriate amount of seating.

Sumbel is a communal event so you need to have at least a couple of people witnessing your promise to fulfil your goal. More than twenty starts becoming unwieldy and can lead to participants losing focus as they listen to others speak. Ideal numbers tend to be around seven to twelve. If your group has grown, then it may be time to divide into two sub-groups to maintain the dedicated focus needed for an effective ritual. The groups can continue to meet between Sumbel events and share ideas, brainstorm, and encourage each other. Sumbel groups, if not family and close friends, should meet on a regular basis (say monthly) to check on progress, develop friendships and basically just socialize. By sitting at Sumbel together you have bound your Wyrds together.

As I said earlier there are three key roles within the Sumbel ritual. The first is the **Sumbel Giver**, who is the host of the Sumbel. In elder days the Sumbel Giver was generally the head of the tribe, clan or family. For those of us using the Sumbel as a goal setting ritual, the host will take on the role of the Sumbel Giver. Their role is to start each round of the Sumbel. The Sumbel Giver acts as the leader of the ritual and it is they who describe the purpose of each round. They are the one who calls those gathered to sit at Sumbel. They open and close the ritual and set the general tone and mood for the Sumbel. The Sumbel Giver is responsible for making sure the room is prepared in advance and ensures that the tools for Sumbel are in place for the Ale-bearer to use. The Sumbel Giver pours the mead from the bowl onto the Earth, preferably near a tree (although a potted plant can suffice if the Sumbel Giver lives in a heavily urbanized environment) at the end of Sumbel. The Sumbel Giver then personally hand washes the tools and packs them away.

The second role is the **Ale-bearer**. Historically the Ale-bearer was female, often the wife of the Sumbel Giver. The reason for this is because the Ale-bearer represents the Norns, those female weavers of Wyrd. This is a sacred role that epitomizes the holiness of women. Make no mistake, the Anglo-Norse believed that women were imbued with holiness. The Roman historian Tacitus remarked on this, saying that the chiefs of the Germanic tribes paid attention to the advice given by their wives. In Beowulf, we see Queen Wealtheow herself taking the role of Ale-bearer and giving advice to those sat at Sumbel. The role of the Ale-bearer is a vital one. First, she fills the horn with mead and gives it to the Sumbel Giver, then she makes her way around all the participants in turn so that each one may speak and drink from the horn. With each participant she speaks words of kindness and encouragement. Traditionally the Ale-bearer didn't make boasts herself, however in modern Heathen practice she may choose to do so. If the Ale-bearer does choose to make boasts herself, then she may choose to speak her oath after the Sumbel Giver or last. Next the Ale-bearer pours the leftover mead into the bowl. She then ladles some of the mead back into the horn before refilling it anew. After that, she passes the horn back to the Sumbel Giver to start the next round. At the end of the fourth round of Sumbel, after emptying the horn into the bowl, the Ale-bearer passes the empty horn to the Sumbel Giver to close the Sumbel.

Finally, we have the **Thyle** (pronounced Thool). The role of the Thyle is to challenge someone who makes a boast during the Sumbel that seems beyond the ability of the participant to achieve. This is not done to put the person down or belittle their goals. It is done to make sure that the person making the boast has clearly thought through the process and understands the level of commitment needed to achieve their goal.

Traditionally, this was done to protect the spiritual luck of the tribe. It was believed by the ancient Anglo-Norse (and their modern Heathen counterparts) that a failed oath would weaken the personal spiritual power of the person who wasn't able to complete their oath. We can see this in those who regularly reach and complete their goals. They have a sense of inner strength and purpose that is inspiring and charismatic. Those who regularly succeed in their goals seem to attract luck and good fortune their way. The Anglo-Norse called this inner spiritual strength Maegan (pronounced may-yen). The Thyle, in challenging the person making the oath, is making sure that the oath-maker has the Maegan needed to complete the task with the skills and planning needed to achieve their goal. In doing so, they help the oath-maker gain confidence in their own abilities and inner fortitude to complete their oath while improving self-esteem and confidence in achieving future goals.

The Thyle tests your resolve and holds you accountable in achieving your oath. The Sumbel Giver can challenge the Thyle when the Thyle makes a boast to achieve a goal. It is well known in motivational circles that the people you surround yourself with shape the kind of person you are and will be. Having a regular Sumbel group encourages each other to succeed, holds each other accountable, works to achieve their own goals, shares their successes and helps each other to achieve their goals. This is the collective Maegan of the group (or tribe) that the ancient Anglo-Norse were acutely aware of. The luck of the group was held to be of greatest importance for the well-being of the individual. The Thyle, in challenging oaths, is also watching out for the collective prosperity of the group and of everyone else in it.

Putting it all Together

Now that we know what a Sumbel is, how it works, what is needed for a successful Sumbel, why we should use this ritual, and when to hold a Sumbel, it is now time to outline the how.

At the pre-arranged date and time, the participants should meet at the home of the Sumbel Giver. You may choose to have a meal beforehand and allow for socialising before the ritual starts. Heathen Kindreds will probably hold a Blot (Blessing) and Husel (ritual feast) before holding their Sumbel. At the appointed time, the Sumbel Giver will call the gathered group to sit at Sumbel. Saying something along the lines of "Now it is time to sit at Sumbel and speak of our deeds into Wyrd's Well."

Everyone then proceeds quietly to the room given over to Sumbel, making sure all technology is off and that they have a copy of their goal and plan handy. Everyone takes a place to sit, with the three Ritual leaders sitting together. When everyone is in place, the Sumbel Giver asks the Ale-bearer to fill the horn to start Sumbel. A reminder is given to the assembled group that Sumbel is a powerful ritual and everyone needs to be respectful and courteous at all times. The person holding the horn has the right to speak and full attention must be given to them. Only the Thyle or Sumbel Giver may challenge boasts being made in the third and fourth round. The Ale-bearer speaks with courtesy, kindness and encouragement as she passes the horn around. Everyone treats her with due reverence as she is the embodiment of the Norns.

After this opening speech, the Ale-bearer fills the horn with Mead, allowing some to overflow from the horn into the bowl. She then raises the horn and asks the Norns to hear the words of those gathered and judge our deeds and oaths as worthy of shaping the Orlog of those gathered. The Ale-bearer passes the horn to the Sumbel Giver who holds the horn aloft (about head height without hiding their face behind the horn). The Sumbel Giver then states, "The first round of Sumbel we honour our Gods or toast to our own might and Maegan." The Sumbel Giver then offers a toast to the God of his choice, takes a sip from the horn and passes the horn back to the Ale-bearer. The Ale bearer passes the horn to the Thyle with some kind words. The Thyle offers their boast to the God of their choice and hands the horn back. This process is repeated until everyone has made their toast to the God of their choice.

The Ale-Giver then empties the horn into the bowl, ladles some of the Mead back into the horn and tops it up with more Mead. She passes the horn to the Sumbel Giver who starts the second round with the following, "The second round of Sumbel we honour our ancestors and heroes." The Sumbel-Giver then makes their boast to the hero or ancestor of their choice. The Ale-bearer passes the horn around as per the first round. She again empties the horn into the bowl and refills it as before.

The horn is given to the Sumbel-Giver who then starts the third round with the words, "The third round is a boast of deeds done, laying them into the Well of Wyrd and sharing our Orlog." The Sumbel Giver then boasts of a deed they have done. The horn is passed back to the Ale-bearer who passes the horn around the assembled folk. She empties and refills the horn as before.

With the horn in hand, the Sumbel-Giver opens the final round with, "The fourth round we make our oaths to achieve our deeds or boast of the deeds of our kith and kin." The Sumbel-Giver makes their oath to achieve their next goal, ending the oath with the words, "May Wyrd weave as she wills." After the horn is passed back to the Ale-Bearer, the Thyle may then challenge the oath made. After the challenge is made and countered, the Ale-Bearer continues going around, pausing after receiving the horn to allow the Thyle to challenge the oath if needed.

When finished with the final round, the Ale-Bearer empties the horn and passes it to the Sumbel Giver. The Sumbel Giver holds up the empty horn and says the following words to close the Sumbel, "We have spoken well in Sumbel, may Wyrd weaves as she will, this Sumbel is at an end." The Sumbel Giver the taps the horn three times.

Afterwards, the Sumbel Giver takes the bowl of Mead and pours it out next to a tree. They then clean the Sumbel tools and put them away. If the group are recording oaths, the Thyle can do this now. When all is done, the participants may relax and enjoy each other's company, asking for help and advice if needed, then head home.

The Power of Ritual and Habit Formation on Goal Setting

Whilst this book is primarily focussed on ritualising your goal setting and developing an Anglo-Norse mindset to achieving goals, I would be remiss if I didn't talk about the act of goal setting itself. There are plenty of good books available on goal setting and habit formation, and we are all familiar the concept of SMART goals. I will not go into detail on such things here. Instead, I will discuss the importance of ritual and habit formation in becoming more successful in achieving your goals.

With goals, we are told to dream big and aim for the stars. They should be so large and audacious that they are scary. Apparently, if they are not big and scary, we will not achieve them. For many, large goals become great burdens. They overwhelm, paralyse and then crush our will power. When we fail, our self-esteem falls, and we start viewing ourselves as failures. The dream goal is so vast and complex that we struggle to comprehend how to get from where we are to where we want to be. The problem is not in the dreaming big or aiming high. The problem is in thinking small.

To achieve any goal, we must work out the little day to day steps which we need to do to reach our goal. If you wish to write a book, for example, you need to commit to writing on your book every day. You need to work out how many words you need to write each day to create the book that you are dreaming of writing, within a specific time frame. Then, you need to create the habit of writing each day. Only when you have created the daily habit that will help you achieve your goal, will you be better able to achieve it. Let us explore an example of a fitness goal of doing 200 push ups a day. First, you need to work out how many you are currently capable of doing. Work out when you are going to do them, where you are going to do the push ups, what will you be doing before you do them, what comes next in your day after doing the push ups, what unexpected events could disrupt your routine and how you are going to work around those unexpected disruptions.

Let us use the push up example to explore goal setting with a Sumbel further. Alfred can currently do five push ups and wants to be able to do 200. Alfred decides to do his pushups first thing in the morning, after he goes to the toilet, upon waking. He will do them on his bedroom floor where he has enough space. After his push ups, he will get dressed and start the rest of his day. Alfred is a stay-at-home single father with two young children. He knows that sometimes they get sick, and one occasionally wets the bed. The eldest has to be at school by 8:45 am. So, on the days that they are sick or have an accident, he will do his push ups after he has gotten his eldest child off to school. Alfred then starts his new morning routine of getting up, going to the toilet, then returning to his bedroom to do his daily push ups.

You can see Alfred has his goal, his daily plan, a habit that he can link his new activity to, and an alternate plan in case things go awry. Alfred attends a Sumbel at his friend Ragnar's house. There, he boasts of his goal to do 200 push ups a day. The Thyle, knowing that Alfred is unfit, challenges his boast. Alfred is ready and lays out his plan as discussed above. The Sumbel group nods their approval at Alfred's reply. The Thyle sees another flaw in Alfred's plan. How is he going to increase the number of push ups? Whoops, the flaw is now clear for all to see in Alfred's plan. Alfred is at a bit of a loss, but Ragnar the Sumbel Giver suggests Alfred improve by at least one percent, per day. Alfred agrees that every Wednesday he will add one push up to his daily routine. The Thyle approves of Alfred's amendment and declares the boast a good one.

You might think that one percent per day is only a small amount and, in reality, it is. After all one percent of Alfred's five push ups is 0.05 or one push up every twenty days. If Alfred is very unfit, adding one push up on day twenty would allow his body nearly three weeks to build up the strength needed to improve. Small gains can lead to long lasting changes. As Alfred improves and reaches ten push ups per day, it will only take ten days to add one push up, at one percent per day. Then at twenty push ups it will take only five days to add the next push up. By the time Alfred reaches 50 push ups, he will need to add one push up every two days to improve by one percent, per day. Small changes that may seem barely noticeable when first started, slowly becomes significant gains over time. At one push up per week, Alfred is actually improving by 20% per week, more than twice the speed of one percent per day (7% per week). If Alfred keeps to his plan when he returns to Sumbel in twelve weeks' time, he should be able to boast that he is doing seventeen push ups per day. This may not seem much, but it is a 340% increase to his original five push ups. The consistent effort will bring steady improvements to Alfred's health and his confidence will continue to improve.

Sumbel meets one of the important criteria in successful goal setting and implementation as described by the Behavioural Insights Team in the UK, making your goal public. According to the BIT, the act of stating a goal publicly creates a greater desire to be consistent. After all, we don't like letting others down or have others think less of us when we fail. Another advantage is that we have a group of people who are willing to hold us accountable in achieving our goals. The BIT states that we are 70% more likely to achieve our goals when we have what they call a commitment referee. Sumbel fills both essential functions in achieving our goals.

Returning to our example of Alfred, we see that he has other criteria in place that the BIT recommends for successful goal achievement. A clear and simple plan, an alternate plan, tying his new behaviour to an existing habit, making a public declaration and a support group. One thing that can further help members of a Sumbel group is writing the goal down.

I suggest that the Thyle record goals in a book kept specifically for this purpose. This can be done after the Sumbel to keep the flow of the ritual going. Everyone should, of course, have written their goals down along with their plan of action. If the group has a book with goals recorded in and signed by the member of the group, then it can act like an extra incentive in being similarly binding like a contract. The ancient Anglo-Norse, by being an oral tribal society, didn't write things down. However, the BIT has found that writing down your goals and creating a 'contract' out of them helps us modern westerners in achieving our goals.

When people think of rituals, they often think of being at church on a Sunday morning. Sometimes, they think of rituals like marriage or tea ceremonies of Japan, China and England. Ritual is a habit that has been super-charged with intentionality, awareness and significance. Rituals can help bring balance, inner peace and tranquillity into your life. They give a sense of order, comfort, permanence and purpose in an otherwise chaotic life. This sense of order, inner peace and harmony can allow you to connect with your inner self so that you can create a life of purpose and meaning. In other words, ritual can help you build a worthy life.

The purpose of religious rituals is to connect with the sacred, the numinous, the spirit world wherein resides the Gods, Ancestors and the various Wights (spirit beings). In this, Sumbel is no different. The first two rounds are dedicated to precisely that. Adding the power of sacral ritual to your goals will give them, and you, an extra boost in universal energy (Maegan) on top of your own passion and sense of purpose. For the religiously minded, it will add the extra sense of commitment as one promises before their Gods and Ancestors to achieve a specific deed.

For the Anglo-Norse Heathen, the strength of Gods and Ancestors called upon is also 'lent' to them to achieve their deed. That is, the Heathen can tap into the Maegan of the God, Goddess or ancestor for that extra empowerment to get through the harder times of achieving their goals. Our ancestors want their descendants (us) to succeed so that the chain of generations can continue to grow healthy, holy and stronger. The Aesir and Vanir want us to succeed so that we can aid them in growing the realms of Yggdrasil, the World Tree.

May Your Gods See You

In this book, I have shared a small glimpse of my personal life, hinting at my struggles for the past dozen or so years. I have shared my successes prior to that and my reflection on the differences between the two times. These reflections gave me the realisation that I was not using the powerful ritual of Sumbel to help me with my goal setting. Nor was I thinking small enough to build the daily habits which I needed to succeed.

I introduced you to the ancient North European tribal cultures that are my inspiration, whose religious practices are the basis of my own. I highlighted the two tribal cultures, the Anglii and the Norse who I am most inspired by. Linking them together to form a shared culture, religion, mindset and name; the Anglo-Norse.

We discussed what it means to live a worthy life based upon the ideals, or Thews, of the Anglo-Norse. Wisdom; learning new things, applying that knowledge in your life and then sharing your knowledge with others. Honour; your self-respect and self-esteem, choosing to live by what is right and Thewful, protecting the health, wholeness and holiness of the chain of generations. Loyalty; being true to yourself, your family and your friends, being true to your purpose in life and your goals and dreams. Generosity; giving gifts to friends and family, sharing what you have. Hospitality; providing food, drink and a place to sleep for guests, being a helpful and courteous guest. Hard-work; getting the tasks of daily living done, working on achieving your goals. Being a Capable Fighter; learn self-defence, train in a martial art or study HEMA. Strength; be strong of mind, body, spirit, having strength of purpose and being healthy to live a worthy life.

We discussed Wyrd and Orlog, the Anglo-Norse concepts of fate. How our fates are based upon the layers of decisions, deeds and actions we have made in the past. We can see that even the deeds of our ancestors have shaped our lives and what we do influences the lives of those around us.

The Anglo-Norse concept of time was introduced, where we learned that the present is shaped by the past and in turn becomes the past. The past lives with us and shapes our lives constantly. That future is based only on the debts and obligations we took on in the past and in the present. We then went on to learn that the Anglo-Norse used a lunar calendar, each month starting with the sighting of the first crescent after the new moon. The turning of the seasons, with each new year starting on the Winter Solstice. We've learned that every eight years they held a great celebration. With that knowledge, we understood that the Equinoxes and Solstices were the ideal time to hold Sumbel, and that goal setting needs to take into account these natural divisions of time; month, season, year, and eight-year cycles of time.

The next three chapters focused on the ritual of Sumbel itself. We learned that Sumbel has four rounds, the first to honour the Gods of the participants, the second round is for remembering our ancestors and heroes, the third round is where we boast of the goals we have completed, with the final round being where we promise to complete a new goal. To perform the Sumbel we need the following tools; a room with seats for everyone, a horn or other drinking vessel, a bowl and ladle, Mead or other drink and a small table to hold the tools. The three positions of leadership during the ritual are the Sumbel-Giver who is the host and directs the ritual. The Ale-Bearer who fills the horn with Mead and passes it to every participant each round of Sumbel and embodies the Norns those weavers of Wyrd. The Thyle who challenges the oaths made in the fourth round making sure participants have a well thought out plan to achieve their goal.

Finally, we discussed how the use of Sumbel adds the power of ritual to goal setting. This is the power of intention, awareness, and significance focused on your goals. Rituals also bring order, comfort, permanence and inner peace to your life, connecting you with the sacred spirit worlds, with your inner self and sense of purpose, also increasing the flow of Maegan (life energy, known as chi to the Chinese). To achieve our goals, we need to focus on the small everyday activities that we need to do in order to successfully complete our goals. Finally, Sumbel meets many of the requirements to successfully complete our goals as researched and promoted by the British Behavioural Insights Team.

I am still a long way from being where I want to be. Now, however, I have a plan which I have outlined in this book. With it I have already succeeded in defeating long-term depression (with a lot of help from my family and support from my SuperDad friends). I have finally married the woman I love in a beautiful Heathen ceremony with a mediaeval theme. We built the tables and chairs ourselves and my wonderful, amazing and awe-inspiring Bec sewed all the outfits for the bridal party. We had a lot of help achieving this goal from family and friends. The publishing of this book is another successful goal completed, with the help from some wonderful friends and encouragement from my family. I am continuing to build a worthy life.

Remember that I can be reached via email, my Facebook author's Page; www.facebook.com/buildaworthylife and please leave a review on Amazon.

I hope that you will join me in building a life of worth. May your Gods see you, and Wyrd weave you opportunities for growth and chances to prove your worth.

References and Further Reading

Coulter, James Hjulka, 2003, Germanic Heathenry: A Practical Guide, 1st Books Library

Eliade, Mircea, 1959, The Sacred and The Profane: The Nature of Religion, Translated by Willard R. Trask, A Harvest Book Harcourt Inc

Gundarsson, Kveldulf Hagan, 2006, Our Troth Vol 1 & 2, second edition, Troth Publications

Helder, Chris, 2016, Useful Belief: Because it's better than positive thinking, Helder Consulting Pty Ltd

Pollington, Stephen, 2003, The Mead-Hall: Feasting in Anglo-Saxon England, Anglo Saxon Books

Sass, Robert, 2017, Saxon Paganism for Today, Lulu.com

Scott, Steve, 2017, Novice to Expert: 6 Steps to Learn Anything, Increase Your Knowledge, and Master New Skills, Oldtown Publishing LLC

Scott, Steve & Rebecca Livermore, 2017, Level Up Your Day: How to Maximise the 6 Essential Areas of Your Daily Routine, Archangel Ink

Service, Owain & Rory Gallagher, 2017, Think Small: the surprisingly simple ways to reach big goals, Micheal O'Mara Books Limited

Stone, M.F. 2014, Goals Suck: Why the Obsession with Goal-Setting is a Flawed Approach to Productivity and Life in General, Archangel Ink

Wodening, Eric, 2011, We Are Our Deeds: The Elder Heathenry – Its Ethics and Thew, second edition, White Marsh Press

Wodening, Swain, 2010, Family Rites for the Germanic Heathen, Wednesbury Shire

- 2008, Hammer of the Gods, Anglo-Saxon Paganism in Modern Times, second edition, Wednesbury Shire

Printed in Poland
by Amazon Fulfillment
Poland Sp. z o.o., Wrocław